Give My Regards to ELWAY...

A CARTOON Tribute to JOHN ELWAY

by drew litton...

JOHNSON BOOKS
BOULDER, COLORADO

Contents

FOR DEBBIE,
with Love.

Foreword

by Shannon Sharpe

One thing you'll always hear players and coaches say is "I never read the papers," or "I don't pay any attention to what is written and said about me." OK, maybe that's true sometimes. But even if we aren't paying attention, we'll find out from friends and loved ones anyway. Good or bad, we get the news pretty quickly.

Some of the strongest messages come from Drew Litton. They say a picture is worth a thousand words. It's certainly true in his case. I have no idea where Drew comes up with his ideas, but we are very lucky in Denver to have one of the best.

I played 14 NFL seasons (14 seasons!!), and 12 in Denver, and Drew has been drawing the Broncos and me for my entire career. He has drawn me with big muscles, big shoulders and a big mouth (I wonder where he came up with that one). He has drawn John Elway with big hair and big teeth, a tall and thin Pat Bowlen, a short and thin Mike Shanahan, and he has even taken some jabs at the media (careful, Drew, they'll get you for that!).

One thing all of his characters have in common is they have just three fingers on each hand!

Whether he's drawing the Broncos, another Denver sports team or a national issue, I'm always interested in looking at his latest work. I always get a kick out of it. I think it's because he can summarize an entire opinion in one picture. It's amazing how often he seems to hit the nail on the head.

One time I was talking about the Super Bowl and the fact a team needs to play great to win it, and I said that greatness at the key time is what separates the field. To illustrate (no pun intended) my point, I said, "That's what they didn't call the great ancient leader 'Alexander the Mediocre.'" Well, there's nothing mediocre about Drew's work either. He's Drew the Great. The guys in the locker room have been known to cut out a cartoon and tape it up in the training room, the equipment room or on a teammate's locker. Usually, one cartoon from Drew is all it takes to get the message across.

I know you join me in looking forward to turning the pages of this book, *Give My Regards to Elway*, and watching one more time as John does all the things that made him John Elway and endeared him to Denver, the Rocky Mountain region and the nation's sports fans. Drew's cartoons capture John happy and sad, injured and healthy, winning and losing (all with just three fingers, of course). Drew shows him starting his career with Dan Reeves, going to those first three Super Bowls and finally winning two Super Bowls with Mike Shanahan. One of my favorite cartoons is the Broncos organizational chart, the one that shows John ... and everybody else below him. Drew Litton's work is like that, too. There are his cartoons, and everybody else is below him.

I am proud of having been John's favorite receiver over our careers, but just think what we could have done if we had been drawn with five fingers on each hand!

Enjoy the book!

A Cartoonist Looks Back

Honker noses. Googly eyes. Ears the size of Dumbo's. And, yes, even teeth. Teeth like the ones we learned to draw at a young age while trying to copy Bugs Bunny off the TV. Those are the things cartoonists dream of.

A decent President? Hogwash. Give us Richard Nixon with jowls like a worn-out bloodhound, a red bulging ski nose and the beady little eyes of a shrew. A winning head coach? Oh, sure, the fans love him. But give a me a guy with a 6-10 record and a nose the size of a melon, and I'll be the one getting flagged 15 yards for excessive celebration.

I arrived in Denver in the fall of 1982, pens and ink in tow, to a sports landscape almost completely barren of honker noses and googly eyes. But soon, thankfully, the Broncos made the trade for John Elway. I remember calling a good friend in El Paso, my hometown, to tell him the news. I told him about the legendary 75-yard throws off the wrong foot, the ability to escape fire-breathing linebackers in a single bound. And the teeth. I think I mentioned the teeth.

"Well, what does this mean?" my friend asked.

"Super Bowls," I answered. "Super Bowls."

Little did I realize that John would eventually make five Super Bowl appearances and win two. I wasn't thinking in terms of Hall of Fame then. But I was aware of two things: I had found my Richard Nixon, and the Bugs Bunny training was about to pay off.

The first John Elway training camp gave birth to The Elway Watch in the *Rocky Mountain News* and Elway updates every 15 minutes on sports talk shows. The hysteria inspired the cartoon on page 25 of a photographer popping out of a toilet bowl as John approached.

The Elway caricature took time. All caricatures do. You have to become familiar with the features and then let them sort of evolve and morph into a character. Soon you are able to whittle away the parts you don't need and accentuate the ones you do.

I knew the teeth were a key (it's the upper lip actually, sort of an Elvis thing that exposes the teeth more), but it took a while to get the nuances of the character. And to be honest, in 1983, I was a rookie, just like John. And I lined up under the guard, artistically at least, a lot more often than John. My early drawings were very rough.

I'm often asked if I know John Elway personally, and what he thinks of the cartoons and the way I draw him. John has always been cordial to me when I see him, but he never has really said much about the cartoons or his caricature. I wonder if he is sometimes sensitive about the teeth. I hope he knows I've never drawn them to make fun of him. I just take the features that stand out to me.

In any case, I am extremely grateful to have been able to draw cartoons during the Elway Era. It was something special.

I'm often asked to name my favorite Elway cartoon. I don't have a single "favorite" cartoon. But of my favorites is the one that captured John's long and frustrating quest for a world championship—the drawing of John peering in Joe Sakic's bedroom window, looking longingly at the Stanley Cup Joe and the Avalanche had just won.

Normally, I'm drawing today for tomorrow. I rarely get ideas ahead of an event. But this idea came to me as several of us in the newsroom were talking about how the Avs looked like a sure bet to capture the Cup.

"Just imagine how Elway will feel if it happens," someone said.

Ping. Light bulb. The image popped into my head almost immediately: Elway at the window like the little boy looking in the store window at the toy he can't have. Sakic sleeping. Cup on the dresser. There it was. Just waiting to be drawn. It was a long two weeks while I anxiously waited for the Avs to come through.

Two years later after returning from the Broncos' win over the Packers in the Super Bowl, my publisher challenged me to reprise the Elway-Sakic image. The Reeves-Elway variation was a natural, considering that John's past Super Bowl disappointments were a big part of their strained relationship. And next to John and his teeth, drawing Reeves and his Napoleonic image was one of the caricatures I most enjoyed. But as much fun as I had placing Reeves on the outside looking in at John and his long-coveted treasure, I sweated it when the two met in the very next Super Bowl.

I didn't want to have to draw it a third time.

John's Super Bowl wins were career highlights for me, too. I attended both, drawing on the spot, scanning them into a laptop computer, colorizing them on the screen and transmitting them back to Denver. One of my favorite Elway cartoons of all time was drawn in San Diego following that first Super Bowl victory. I was struggling for the right image if the Broncos were to beat the Packers. I envisioned all the great Super Bowl quarterbacks of the past carrying him off the field. I felt it captured his long journey to finally win the Lombardi Trophy.

I have continued to draw John even after retirement. His election to the Pro Football Hall of Fame provided me the opportunity to salute not only his great career but also the place he will always occupy as the ultimate leader of Denver's professional football team. That's what I hope the image of him leading Randy Gradishar and Floyd Little into the Hall with him conveys on page 126.

So here are a few of the Elway cartoons I've drawn over the years. I hope you have as much fun reminiscing with them as I did drawing them. John's entire career was truly amazing.

In years to come, it may even seem almost like a fairy tale, a story you might tell your children at bedtime ...

Acknowledgments

I'm thankful to so many people who played a part in this collection. It has been some 20 years in the making, and so many wonderful friends, colleagues and editors have helped to bring it to fruition.

First, I'd like to thank my incredible wife, Debbie, whose strength, faith and encouragement have been such an inspiration to myself and so many others. She is, without a doubt, the greatest gift God has ever blessed me with.

Thanks to John Temple, the best editor any cartoonist could ever dream of. And to the late Ralph Looney, who believed.

To Barry Forbis and Kevin Huhn, the best sports editors in the country. And to Dave Reid and Mike Madigan, who paved the way.

To Denny Dressman, whom I admire so much and am forever grateful to for seeing beyond the product and believing in the potential.

To Mira Perrizo, Robert Sheldon, and Stephen Topping at Johnson Books.

To Don Pavlin for his incredible work on this book and everyone in Shared Work for the always remarkable scans.

To Shannon Sharpe for taking the time to meet a tight deadline on the Foreword, and to Jim Saccomano of the Denver Broncos for making it happen.

And, of course, to John Elway for the years of memorable moments and for the cartoons that resulted from them.

To Gary Rakowsky, the most amazing computer tech guy on the entire planet.

To Brian Clark for the magical cover fixes. To Bob, Colleen, Webb, Richard, Tim, Mike, Chuck M., Chuck H., Angel, Paul and Josephine for spell-checking the word balloons. And to Steve Foster, Brian MacQueen, Lori Montoya, Taylor, Micaela and Mr. Clark once again for getting Win, lose & Drew onto the page every day.

To Fred, Wolfie, Marc, Mr. Littwin, Michael, Sam, Dean, Scott, Gerry, Diane, Tom, Steve O. and George for making the newsroom "cartoonist friendly."

To Meredith Worden, Norm Clarke, Mike and Debbie Minter, Larry and Linda Kapke, Kevin and Mary Wood, Bob and Pat Lovelace, Chris Courtney, Tom and Sherry Assmus, Mike Melick, the Pettits, the Jensens, Jerry Hoggatt and Ron Achenbach for the years of treasured friendship. Long live the Calamaris.

To Dr. Ed Eigner for being the very best. And Lance Armstrong for the book of encouragement. To Bill and Jan Oudemolen, and Ken Kelly for love, prayer, and guidance.

To my father, Laveron, who continues to be a shining example of "overcoming adversity." And Mom, who shines right along with him. To Gary and Allan, the most fantastic brothers of all. To my wonderful sisters, Charlie, Judy, Lynn and T.J. And to the Kitchell family for making me feel like I belong.

And mostly, to Jesus, whose depth of love is still unfathomable, whose grace is truly amazing and whose hope is never ending. Thank you for this gift to cartoon for a living.

© 2004 Denver Publishing Company / *Rocky Mountain News*
ISBN 1-55566-356-7
Published by Johnson Books, 1880 S. 57th Court, Boulder, CO 80301
e-mail: books@jpcolorado.com   www.johnsonbooks.com

An Amazing Athlete

May 29, 2003

December 3, 1991

November 26, 1996: An Elway pass bounces off several defenders and into the hands of Ed McCaffrey to win a thriller against the Vikings.

October 1, 1991: Elway bowls over several Vikings defenders for a Broncos win.

December 14, 1993

February 2, 1999

March 5, 2000

March 27, 1983: These early drawings are extremely rough. I was just beginning to learn the craft. Elway lined up under one of his guards one Sunday, rather than his center. I lined up under a guard every day for about two years.

May 4, 1983

May 5, 1983

July 12, 1983

June 1983

Drew Litton's "Give My Regards to Elway"
A look at a day in the life of a Phenomenon!!

July 14, 1983: These three pages were all part of a sketchbook I did at Elway's first camp. They are just that—right out of the sketch book. I didn't turn them into final drawings. I think they still capture the essence of Elway's (and my) first trip to Greeley.

July 14, 1983

July 14, 1983

August 7, 1983

August 26, 1983

September 25, 1983: Elway started the season but was quickly benched for Steve DeBerg. It wouldn't last long.

November 8, 1983: Elway had his job back. He would never relinquish it for the rest of his career.

September 9, 1984: Michael Jackson makes a concert appearance at Mile High Stadium. Which got me thinking of the parallels.

September 1984

October 1984

October 28, 1984: Elway's shoulder injury becomes an epic event.

October 20, 1985

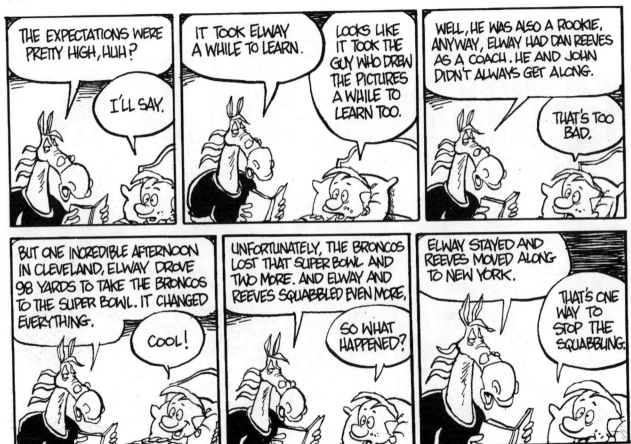

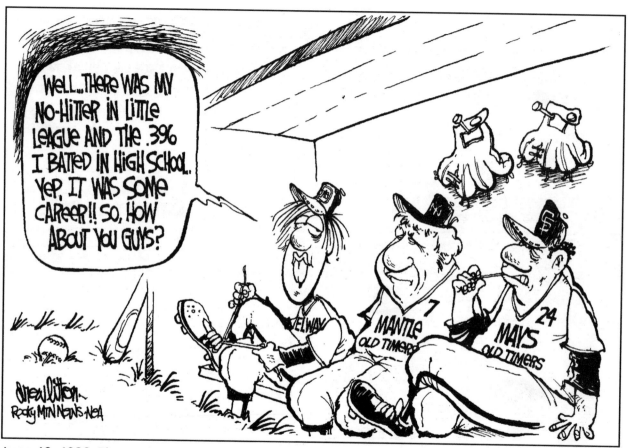

June 12, 1986: Elway plays in an old-timers baseball game at Mile High.

October 2, 1986

January 5, 1987

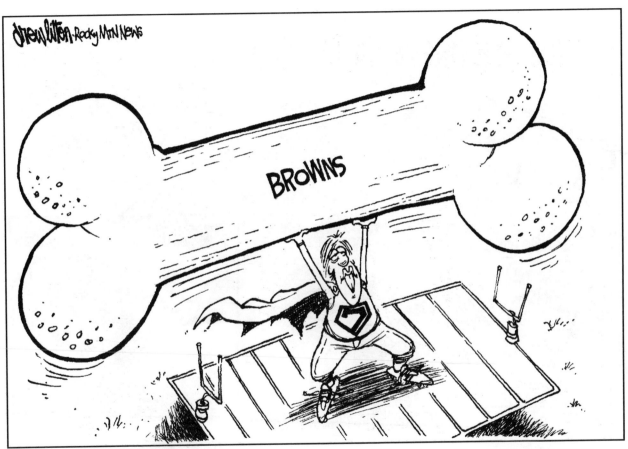

January 12, 1987: Elway defeats the Browns in the AFC title game with what has become known as The Drive.

January 13, 1987

January 13, 1987

December 18, 1986

January 31, 1988: Elway makes a second straight Super Bowl appearance.

THE DENVER BRONCOS SUPER BOWL TEAM PICTURE

January 1988: The results are the same. The Broncos lose to the Redskins.

September 1988: Brian Bosworth becomes Elway's arch rival.

October 1988

May 31, 1989

September 1989

September 22, 1989

October 4, 1989

November 2, 1989: This was inspired by a name Brian Bosworth had called Elway.

December 24, 1989

November 20, 1990

August 11, 1991: The Broncos toy with letting Elway call the plays.

January 5, 1992: Elway leads yet another miraculous comeback to defeat Houston 26–24 in the playoffs.

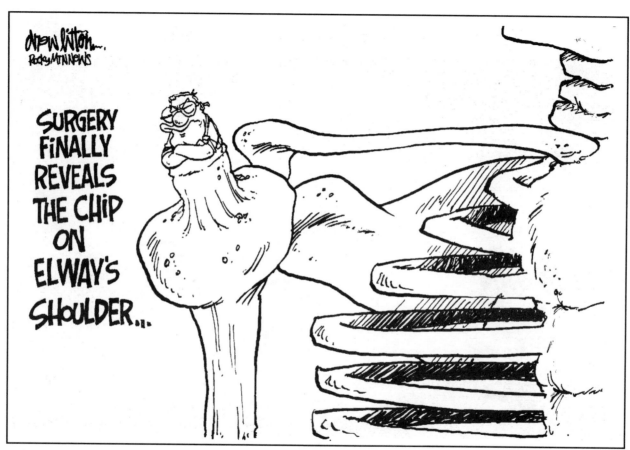

February 16, 1992

THE EAGLES DEFENSE SURVEYS JOHN ELWAY...

September 20, 1992

October 6, 1992

November 8, 1992: Elway completes the first half of a disappointing season, only to face the second half.

November 10, 1992

December 6, 1992

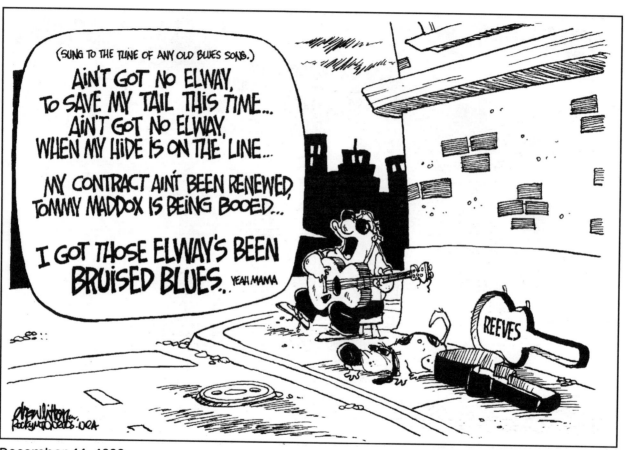

December 11, 1992

December 15, 1992: Elway comes back from injuries a bit too late.

Time for Some Color

September 14, 1993

September 19, 1993

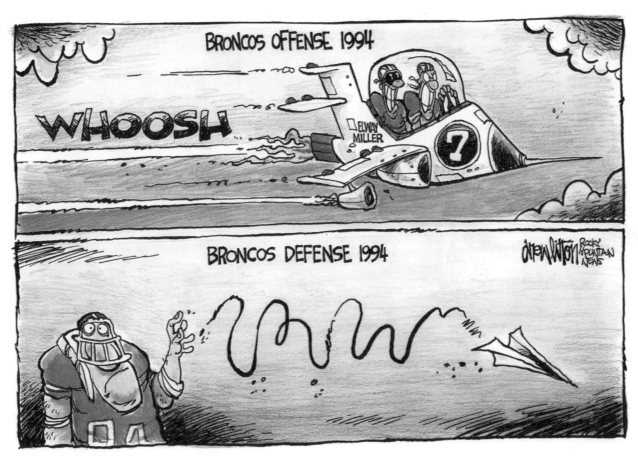

March 25, 1994

September 23, 1994

June 16, 1996: This was drawn after the Avalanche won the Stanley Cup.

November 6, 1996

January 12, 1997: The heavily favored Broncos lose a playoff game to the Jacksonville Jaguars.

January 26, 1998: The Broncos defeat the Packers 31–24 in Super Bowl XXXII for John's first championship.

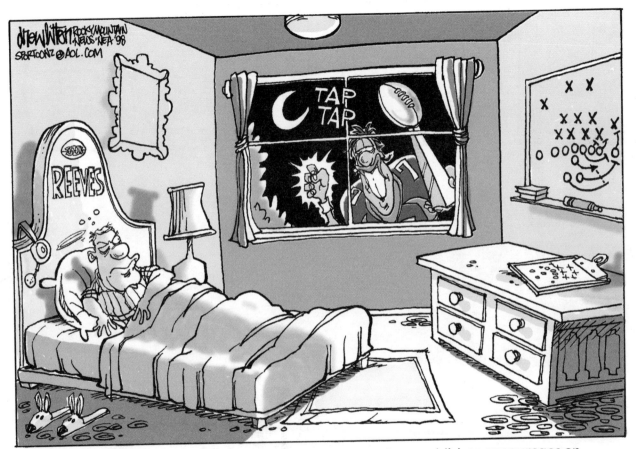

February 1, 1998: After the Broncos win the Super Bowl my publisher encourages an Elway-Sakic update.

October 6, 1998

November 10, 1998

November 15, 1998

December 8, 1998

January 18, 1999: Elway goes to his second Super Bowl in a row, only to face an old nemesis.

January 17, 1999

Unpublished: This cartoon is a Hall of Fame tribute I presented to John Elway at halftime of a Crush game.

August 29, 1993

July 27, 1993

September 5, 1993

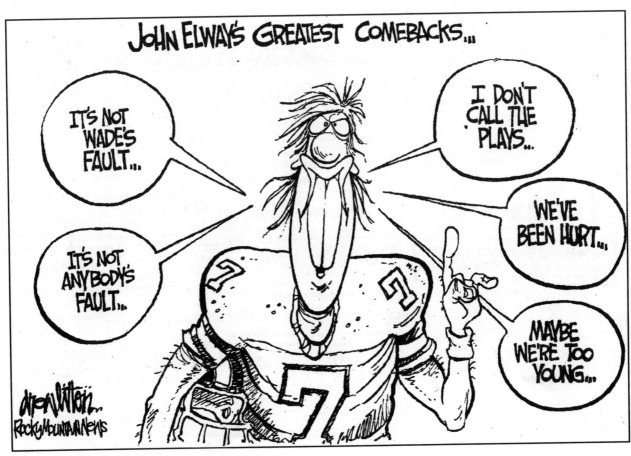

December 8, 1993

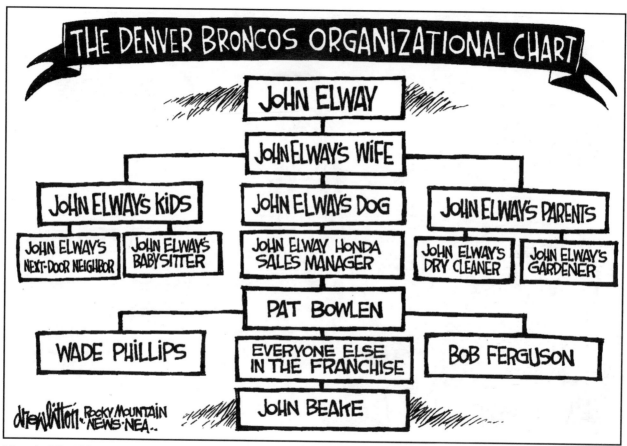

March 23, 1994: This is one of my better-known Elway cartoons. It kind of summed it all up.

April 26, 1994

August 16, 1994

August 28, 1994

September 7, 1994: Elway starts poorly against the Chargers in the season opener. It was an omen for the 1994 season. The Broncos finished 7–9.

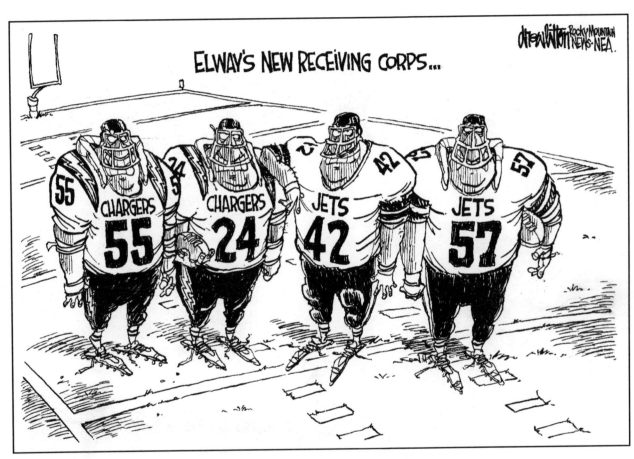

September 13, 1994

September 28, 1994

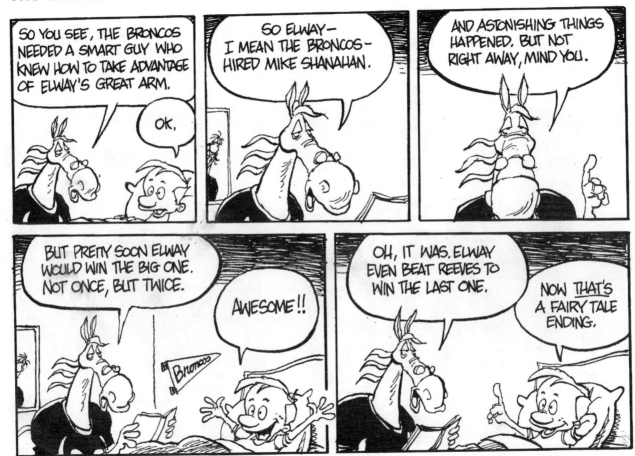

January 13, 1995

January 29, 1995

February 2, 1995

October 24, 1995: Elway was fine with Kryptonite. But cold weather was a whole different matter.

December 21, 1995

August 25, 1996

August 6, 1997

September 9, 1997

January 5, 1998

January 12, 1998: Elway returns to give the Super Bowl another try. This time things turn out better—the Broncos beat the Packers, and Elway wins his first title.

DECISIONS, DECISIONS...

April 9, 1998: Elway contemplates retirement but finally decides against it.

June 1, 1998

August 3, 1998

August 5, 1998: Elway's all-pro left guard opts to retire. John still hopes he'll return.

November 24, 1998

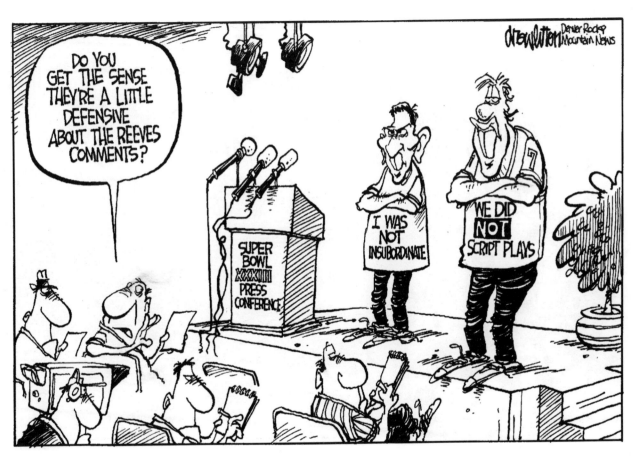

January 25, 1999

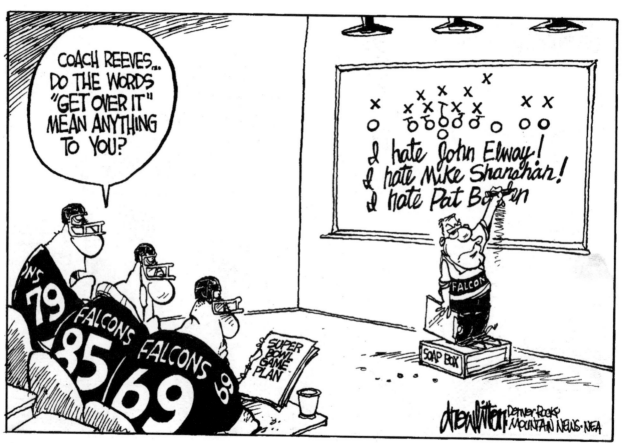

January 26, 1999

January 31, 1999

February 1, 1999: The Broncos capture their second straight Super Bowl with a 34–19 win over the Falcons and Dan Reeves.

Out of Pads and Into the Hall of Fame

EVENTUALLY ALL GOOD THINGS MUST END.

BUT I DON'T WANT TO GO TO SLEEP YET.

OK. HEY, WANT TO LEARN TO DRAW JOHN ELWAY?

YEAH. CAN I? REALLY?

SURE. FIRST WE START WITH THE CHIN. THAT LEAVES A LOT OF ROOM...

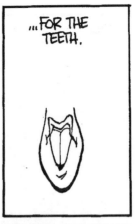

...FOR THE TEETH.

NEXT IS THE NOSE AND EARS; NOTHING SPECIAL.

THEN THE EYES. THEY'RE KIND OF LIKE GARFIELD THE CAT'S.

ELWAY ALWAYS LOOKS SLEEPY-TOO MANY YEARS WITH REEVES, I THINK.

THEN THE HAIR. THE MESSIER THE BETTER.

THEN YOU FINISH IT OFF.

SPEAKING OF FINISH, LET'S SEE HOW THE STORY ENDS.

February 12, 1999

April 7, 1999

April 25, 1999: Elway finally decides to retire.

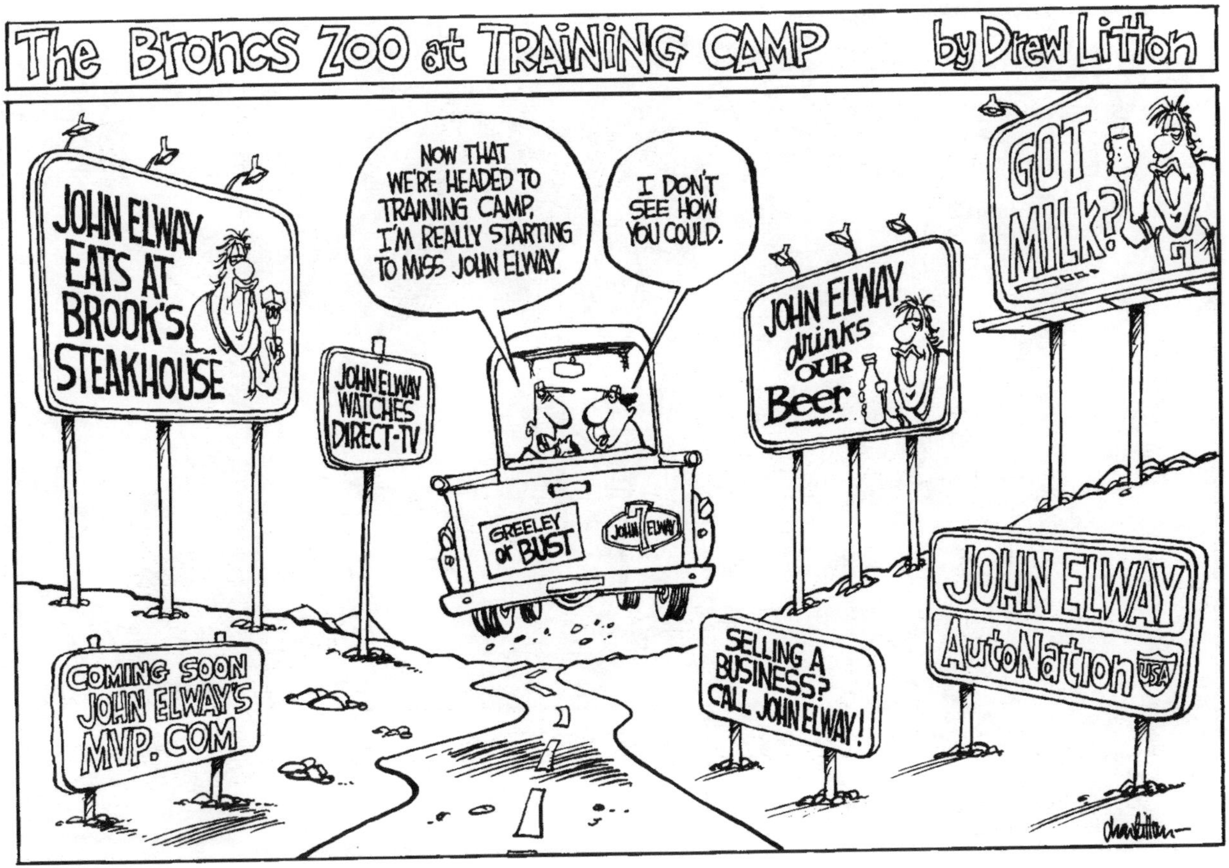

August 15, 1999

September 14, 1999

September 21, 1999

October 24, 1999

July 20, 2000

July 12, 2002

June 20, 2002: John begins his association with arena football.

January 11, 2003

February 8, 2003

January 26, 2004: John Elway is elected to the Pro Football Hall of Fame on the first ballot.

Conclusion

About the Cartoonist

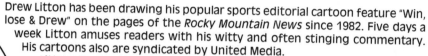

Drew Litton has been drawing his popular sports editorial cartoon feature "Win, lose & Drew" on the pages of the *Rocky Mountain News* since 1982. Five days a week Litton amuses readers with his witty and often stinging commentary. His cartoons also are syndicated by United Media.

Litton attended the University of Texas at El Paso, where he developed his warped sense of humor about sports while watching the UTEP football program. Born and raised in El Paso, Litton began his career at the *El Paso Times* before moving on to the *News* to become one of the nation's few full-time sports cartoonists. His cartoons have appeared in *Sports Illustrated*, *The Sporting News*, *USA Today*, and the *New York Times*. In 1994 the National Cartoonists Society honored him with a Reuben award for sports cartooning.

His originals and limited-edition lithographs are available at the Fascination St. Gallery in Cherry Creek or online at Fascinationst.com.

Give My Regards to Elway is published by Johnson Books in cooperation with the *News*. It is Litton's third cartoon collection. *Greatest Hits*, published in 1987, and *Win, lose and Drew*, published in 1997, are no longer available.

Drew and his wife, Debbie, reside along with their three biscuit-starved dogs in Littleton, Colorado.